THANK YOU

for everything !

from : ____________________

to : ____________________

date :

D1715192

Made in the USA
Monee, IL
20 June 2022

98317603R00065